Everybody Has Something to Give

Written by

Monica Ashour, MTS, M Hum

Illustrated by

Marilee Harrald-Pilz

Pauline
BOOKS & MEDIA
Boston

Library of Congress Cataloging-in-Publication Data

Ashour, Monica.

Everybody has something to give / written by Monica Ashour, MTS, M Hum ; illustrated by Marilee Harrald-Pilz.

pages cm

Summary: "This book helps children see themselves and others as gifts, explores giving and receiving in love, and shows how the gift of self is made through the body"-- Provided by publisher.

ISBN 978-0-8198-2389-2 (soft cover) -- ISBN 0-8198-2389-9 (soft cover)

1. Gifts--Religious aspects--Christianity--Juvenile literature. 2. Self--Religious aspects--Catholic Church--Juvenile literature. I. Harrald-Pilz, Marilee. II. Title.

BR115.G54A84 2015

248.8′2--dc23

2014046154

Cover and interior design by Mary Joseph Peterson, FSP

Published by Pauline Books & Media, 50 Saint Pauls Avenue, Boston, MA 02130–3491

Printed in U.S.A.

EHSG VSAUSAPEOILL2-1710035 2389-9

www.pauline.org

1 2 3 4 5 6 7 8 9 19 18 17 16 15

Note to Parents, Guardians, and Teachers

For Saint John Paul II, the gift of self is the meaning of life. Further, the gift of self is a "code" for the reason we all exist: love! Since the word *love* is often used in misleading ways, *Everybody Has Something to Give* clearly defines the Christian understanding of love. One's self is not a *thing* given to show love. Human beings—body and soul—give the gift of self by bodily presence and actions. Each of us is a *person* who loves by giving him or her self through our bodies.

It's important for adults to communicate that the gift of self takes two forms: giving and receiving. Both are ways of being a gift. Children will begin to see that it is not demeaning to receive from another. On the other hand, one need not *only* receive; everyone can initiate the gift of self. With true giving and receiving, a strong bond is formed. This is what Saint John Paul II calls a "communion of persons." It reflects Christianity itself—a fruitful communion of persons.

The loving dialogue of giving and receiving is modeled for us by Jesus Christ. Because the Son of God became human—body and soul—we are able to see that the purpose of our bodies is love. May we all learn to say, "This is my body" with Jesus and his Mother, Mary.

For more information and teaching ideas for this and other Theology of the Body principles, please visit www.pauline.org/tob4children.

Big boxes, little bags, wrapping paper, ribbons, bows, and a card: gifts come in all colors and shapes and sizes.

Everyone has something to give—even when it isn't a birthday or Christmas or some other special day.

But we don't just give something wonderful in a box or bag or wrapping paper with lots of sticky tape.

When we give a gift, we give ourselves, too.

I have something to give.

When I give a gift, I also give myself.

I *am* a gift.

I give myself with my body.

It's a gift when I brush my sister's hair,

or push my little brother on the swing,

or help Dad wash the car,

or set the table for Mom.

It’s a gift when I sing happy birthday
to my cousin.

It’s a gift when I draw a picture for Grandma,

and when I smile at you.

Other people have something to give.

When others give a gift to me, they give themselves, too.

They *are* gifts.

They give themselves to me with their bodies.

It's a gift when my sister plays a game with me, and we take turns, and I get to be blue;

or when my little brother holds my hand;

or when Dad
carries me piggyback
all the way up the stairs and into my room;

and when Mom pulls up the zipper on
my jacket when it gets stuck.

It’s a gift when my cousin shows me
how to throw the ball before it rains;

when Grandma bakes my favorite cookies;

and you smile at me.

We all have something to give.

And we all receive gifts.

When we receive a gift, we also give ourselves.

We receive others' gifts with our bodies.

It's a gift when I play with my sister and
keep taking turns until the game is over;

or when I squeeze my little brother's hand,
but not too hard;

or when I ride
on Daddy's back
and hold on tight so I don't fall off;

and when I put
my chin up
and wait for Mom
to zip my jacket.

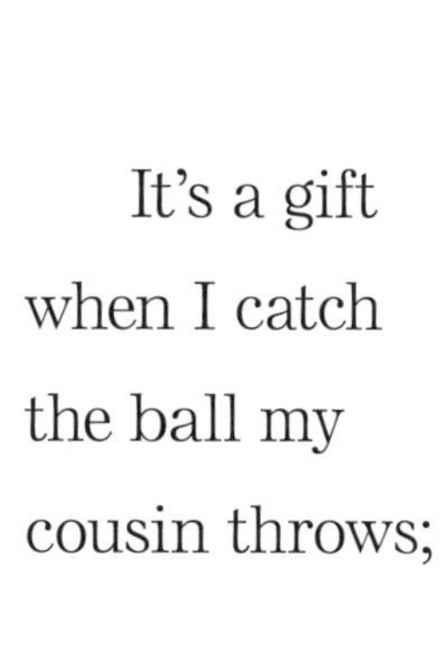

It’s a gift
when I catch
the ball my
cousin throws;

when I have cookies and milk in Grandma’s kitchen;

and when you smile back at me.

We are gifts. Who leaves a gift unopened?

We all tear the paper and peel off the tape. We can't wait to see what's inside!

And when we do, we grow closer to each other.

Games and piggyback rides and zippers and catch and holding hands and cookies and smiling make sisters and dads and moms and cousins and brothers and grandmas and you and me grow closer.

We grow closer to each other with our bodies.

Petting Zoo
FUN HOUSE
COTTON CANDY

But not just sisters and dads and moms and cousins and brothers and grandmas and you and I are gifts.

Jesus is a gift, too. Jesus has something to give.

He gives himself to us.

Jesus gives himself with his body.

His hands healed. His ears heard.

His voice forgave. He walked to meet us.

He searched to find us. He died on a cross to save us. He did all these things with his body.

Jesus still gives himself to us. He says, "This is my Body, given for you."

Jesus wants us to open his gift.

When we receive Jesus, we give ourselves.

We give ourselves to Jesus with our bodies when we let him heal us, when we let him speak to us, when we let him forgive us, when we let him walk to meet us, when we let him find us, when we let him save us.

We give ourselves to Jesus when we give ourselves to others.

We give ourselves to Jesus when we receive others.

Giving and receiving is how we say "Amen" with our bodies.

Then, we are close to Jesus and to others!

Jesus is a gift. You are a gift. I am a gift.

We give with our bodies.

We receive with our bodies.

We grow close to one another with our bodies.

With our bodies, we open the gift of love.

Everyone has something to give.

Monica Ashour

National speaker, former teacher, and executive director of the Theology of the Body Evangelization Team (TOBET), Monica Ashour makes the depth and breadth of Saint John Paul II's revolutionary Theology of the Body (TOB) accessible. Building on her **TOB for Tots** series, Monica, who holds two master's degrees from the University of Dallas in the humanities and theological studies, goes one step deeper in **TOB for Kids**. These books make the mystery of the human person visible in the context of Catholic faith. Young and old alike will learn to see the BODY rightly: as a gift from God and a call to love. For more resources from TOBET, go to www.tobet.org.

Marilee Harrald-Pilz

Marilee Harrald-Pilz has been working as a freelance illustrator since 1979. After graduating from the University of Illinois with a BA in art education, she attended the Chicago Academy of Art, the American Academy of Art, and the School of the Art Institute of Chicago. A proud member of the Picture Book Artists Association, Marilee has primarily focused on the illustration of books, educational materials, magazines, and greetings cards for children. As a senior illustrator at Diamond Toy Company, she illustrated licensed characters, packaging, and display cards. Marilee has also worked as a designer of educational products at Cook Communications Ministries and Scripture Press Publications.

Marilee's work can be seen at:
www.MarileeHarrald-Pilz.com,
and www.storybookartsinc.com

Our Positively Human Line offers an affirmative view of the human person while integrating faith concepts for kids.

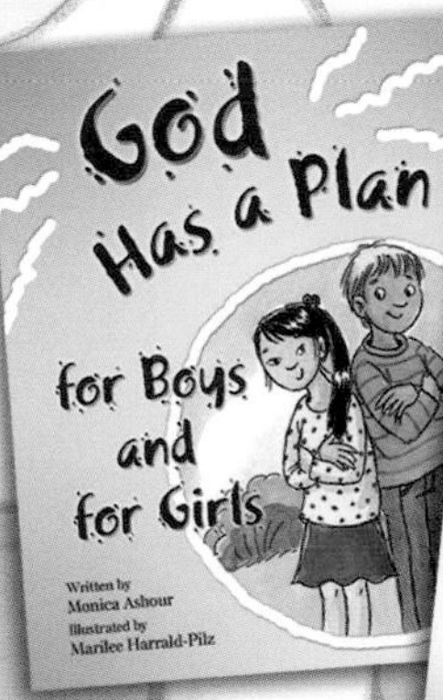

Coming Soon!

Mommy, Am I Strong?
Daddy, Am I Beautiful?

To find these and other delightful books for children, visit one of our Pauline Books & Media centers listed at the end of this book or stop by: www.pauline.org. We'd love to hear from you!

Tales and Legends from
Pauline kids
The 3 Trees
Adapted by Gabriel Ringlet
Illustrated by Daniella Oh
The Little Lost Lamb
Written and Illustrated by Geri Berger Haines
the QUEEN & the CROSS
The Story of Saint Helen
Written by Cornelia Mary Bilinsky
Illustrated by Rebecca Stuhff
SANTA'S Secret Story
Written by Cornelia Mary Bilinsky
Illustrated by Candace Camling
The Saint Who Fought the Dragon
The Story of Saint George
Written by Cornelia Mary Bilinsky
Illustrated by Theresa Brandon

Who are the Daughters of St. Paul?

We are Catholic sisters. Our mission is to be like Saint Paul and tell everyone about Jesus! There are so many ways for people to communicate with each other. We want to use all of them so everyone will know how much God loves us. We do this by printing books (you're holding one!), making radio shows, singing, helping people at our bookstores, using the Internet, and in many other ways.

Visit our Web site at www.pauline.org

The Daughters of St. Paul operate book and media centers at the following addresses. Visit, call, or write the one nearest you today, or find us at www.pauline.org.

CALIFORNIA
3908 Sepulveda Blvd, Culver City, CA 90230 — 310-397-8676
935 Brewster Avenue, Redwood City, CA 94063 — 650-369-4230
5945 Balboa Avenue, San Diego, CA 92111 — 858-565-9181

FLORIDA
145 SW 107th Avenue, Miami, FL 33174 — 305-559-6715

HAWAII
1143 Bishop Street, Honolulu, HI 96813 — 808-521-2731

ILLINOIS
172 North Michigan Avenue, Chicago, IL 60601 — 312-346-4228

LOUISIANA
4403 Veterans Memorial Blvd, Metairie, LA 70006 — 504-887-7631

MASSACHUSETTS
885 Providence Hwy, Dedham, MA 02026 — 781-326-5385

MISSOURI
9804 Watson Road, St. Louis, MO 63126 — 314-965-3512

NEW YORK
64 West 38th Street, New York, NY 10018 — 212-754-1110

SOUTH CAROLINA
243 King Street, Charleston, SC 29401 — 843-577-0175

TEXAS
Currently no book center; for parish exhibits or outreach evangelization, contact: 210-569-0500 or SanAntonio@paulinemedia.com

VIRGINIA
1025 King Street, Alexandria, VA 22314 — 703-549-3806

CANADA
3022 Dufferin Street, Toronto, ON M6B 3T5 — 416-781-9131

SMILE God Loves you!